THE CHOICE IS YOURS.

THAT IS THE CORE PHILOSOPHY OF THE MINDFUL LIFE COLLECTION CREATED BY JAE ELLARD. The choice is yours to start anywhere, at any point in your life, to create more awareness around the choices you make each day that either support or sabotage your desired outcome to create meaningful engagement and sustainable balance between the interconnected roles, relationships, and responsibilities that make up your life.

The Mindful Life collection includes four books to generate awareness, reflection, and conversation.

Stop & Think: Creating New Awareness is about the choices you have and your understanding of the impact of those choices.

Stop & See: Developing Intentional Habits is about your ability to consciously choose to create habits that support your definitions of balance and success.

Stop & Listen: Practicing Presence is about working with your choices to create deeper engagement with self, others, and your environment.

Beyond Tips & Tricks: Mindful Management is about leading groups to take accountability for making and accepting choices.

WHAT DOES IT MEAN TO BE PRESENT?

People talk about this concept quite a bit, but what does it really mean to be present? Is it a feeling, a perception, a way of life, a state of mind, all of the above?

This book will explore what it means to be present at work and how your choices can help you create deeper engagement with your environment, others, and yourself. Through this content, you will understand your ability to intentionally create deeper presence in your life.

WHAT IS PRESENCE?

Creating presence is pretty simple once you are clear on what it is you are trying to create. Simple, however, does not always mean easy.

Presence can mean different things to different people. Some call it wakefulness, attention, consciousness, connection, or engagement. Whichever words you choose, the underlying meaning is the same.

Presence is the ability to experience the moment in time that is not the past or the future, but is right now – like the moment you just read this sentence. That is experiencing presence.

If presence were easy to find and maintain, then there would not be much to say beyond "Be in the moment." As you may already be aware, it's a bit more complicated to connect into a specific moment, let alone a series of moments or even an entire day of moments.

There is so much to explore on this topic. There are hundreds of books with thousands of years of thought leaders' ideas and notions on ways to be present, types of presence, and methods for creating presence.

This book is a mash-up of old wisdom and new thinking overlaid onto everyday pressures and expectations encountered at work. It's about distilling information, experiences, and best practices into something relevant and easily actionable for any person regardless of job type, job level, or geographic location.

The practice of presence at work includes your relationship with your environment (especially the technology in your environment) as well as your relationships with others, as most people do not work alone (even people who work alone in the literal sense still have to work with others). Last, presence includes being present in your relationship with yourself.

What does presence really mean in today's world of work?

For most people, presence means the ability to live in the moment with minimal distraction disrupting or interfering with that moment.

At work, this translates to the ability to connect, engage, create, and maybe even complete the task at hand, free of the disruptions that can come from your environment, from others, and from within.

THIS IS WHERE IT GETS TRICKY

Interruptions and distractions come every day, hour, and second from a zillion different places.

They come from technology – all the buzzes, chimes, chirps, and vibrations from a menagerie of devices all within arm's reach, each with their own data and demands to be answered or acknowledged.

They come externally from others. Perhaps a person says or does something that pulls you out of your focus or disrupts connection to your feelings in a particular moment.

Interruption and distraction also come from within. Your senses – for example, the smell of cookies or a sensation like feeling the sun – can pull you out of a moment. And interruption and distraction come from your thoughts, the chatter, the little voice in your head that accompanies you all day long wherever you go – to a meeting, to the store, to home, even to bed.

It is a simple fact that we live in a world filled with disruption.

WHICH BRINGS US TO CHOICE.

These interruptions and distractions can be negative (like a phone buzzing) or positive (like the smell of cookies). Either way, the impact is the same – you experience a moment of disengagement with whatever it is that you are doing.

In many ways, "negative" and "positive" are relative when it comes to distractions. The smell of cookies may remind you of your grandmother, giving you a pleasant feeling by recalling a memory. Or your phone buzzing may remind you that your manager is waiting for you to accomplish a task, which may bring up fear of what may happen in the future if you do not complete the request in time.

Your ability to experience being present boils down to how you choose to respond to all types of interruptions, both negative and positive.

Practicing presence begins the moment you accept accountability for all the choices you make in a single day that can either support or sabotage your desired outcomes to create deeper connection and engagement with your environment, others, and self.

There is more to know before we get to some techniques for practicing presence. It is helpful to explore two other closely related concepts, balance and awareness.

BALANCE

Just like the definition of presence, balance can mean many things to people. Balance can be about work-life, workload as well as energy.

It doesn't matter what you call "balance," just like it doesn't matter what you call presence. Many people call balance different things – harmony, integration, blur, flexibility.

No matter what words you use, the intended outcome is the same: to create easy joy and meaningful engagement (presence) between the interconnected relationships, roles, and responsibilities that make up your life.

When it comes to balance, no two people share the same idea or have the same need for balance, because **balance is something different to everyone.**

It's also important to know (and accept) that you will be in and out of balance your entire life as your life shifts and changes. The meaning of balance changes over time for each person as one's values in life shift with age and through different life experiences.

The common elements that contribute to or diminish your state of balance include being aware of and communicating your values via your words and actions, understanding how you use your time and how you respond to stress, and setting boundaries to hold it all together.

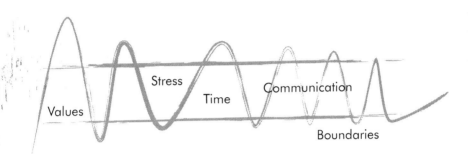

Values Stress Time Communication Boundaries

**THE SAME IS TRUE FOR PRESENCE
AS IT IS FOR BALANCE.**

When it comes to feeling and being present, each person has his or her own idea of what is desirable, acceptable, and comfortable. You will flow in and out of presence, and experience different levels of presence your entire life as moments shift and change around you and as your skills to cultivate presence deepen and grow.

AWARENESS

Awareness, which is a core element of presence, is a deceptively simple concept to understand, and a multilayered skill to develop. This book and the Mindful Life Program are based on the Awareness Framework.

AWARENESS IS THE ABILITY TO **SEE THE WORLD** AND HOW **YOU SHOW UP** IN IT.

The Awareness Framework is built on the idea that behavior has an impact and that there is a result, whether intentional or unintentional, related to the behavior.

When people choose to or are empowered to become more aware of their **behavior**, they are able to be more accountable in their roles and to their teams, more authentic in their communication, and more awake (more present) in their environment (both literally and figuratively).

The **impact** to the team and organization is a shift in the team's ability to be more innovative and more productive on multiple levels. The **result** is sustainable success, both for teams and for individuals.

When you have a framework to begin to understand awareness, you are able to build it as a skill, just like listening or communication.

THE AWARENESS FRAMEWORK

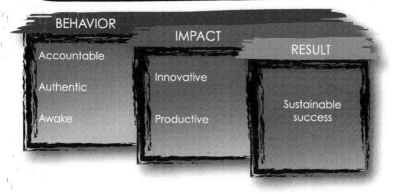

BEHAVIOR

Accountable

Authentic

Awake

IMPACT

Innovative

Productive

RESULT

Sustainable success

AWARENESS IS A SKILL

Awareness – your ability to see the world and how you show up in it – is a skill. Just like learning math, you learn awareness in different layers that build on each other.

First you have to learn addition and subtraction before you can learn multiplication and division, then you move into algebra, calculus, and statistics. You can't start learning math at a statistics level (well, you can try, but odds are you won't get very far).

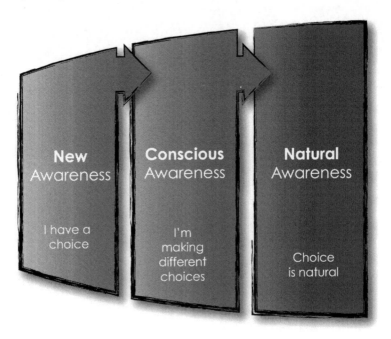

New awareness is about taking an inventory of your world and understanding the impact of your behavior on the world around you and within you – things like what makes you happy, sad, and stressed. New awareness is where you become aware you have choices.

Conscious awareness is being more conscious about what it is you are seeing around you and understanding it at a deeper level. It's the place of knowing you have choices. Some days you might make choices that sabotage your desired outcomes for balance and success, and other days you might make choices that support your desired outcomes. Both ways you choose and you are aware that it is a choice.

Natural awareness is where you fully see your behavior patterns and internalize making choices that support your desired outcome for balance and success. This is where balance has become a lifestyle or a habit and feels natural.

It is through the skill of awareness that you can begin to understand where and when you are distracted or disengaged from your environment, others, and yourself.

Awareness is your ability to see the world and how you show up in it. This includes seeing when you are not showing up and your ability to notice the types of interruptions and distractions that have the greatest impact on your ability to stay engaged.

In the same way that awareness is a skill, so is presence – and the same levels apply.

New presence is your ability to pay attention to whether you are engaged in the moment.

Conscious presence is when you intentionally choose to engage or disengage from the moment.

Natural presence happens when you are engaged and have awareness around your distraction triggers that have the potential to pull you out of a moment.

Now that you have a better understanding of what presence is and how it relates to balance and awareness, it can be simple to create deeper engagement at work.

(Okay, maybe not simple, but at least the path is getting a bit more defined.)

PRESENCE

OBVIOUS

There are three areas in which you can practice presence that will have a direct impact to your level of engagement in any workplace: practicing presence with your environment, with others, and with yourself.

Not surprisingly, they all start with you and having awareness around the choices you make each day.

With many of the choices you make each day, it is quite obvious that they will not create engagement. For example, when you multitask in a meeting, when you dismiss a coworker when they share something personal with you, when you chat on instant messaging while on a conference call, or when you ignore that little voice inside – these are all examples of workplace disengagement and also common examples of ways people are disconnected at work.

NOT SO OBVIOUS

With other choices you make each day, the impact of disengagement is not so obvious. This includes things like staying perpetually busy and focused on activities without clear outcomes, blaming and criticizing others, or working all day with no attention paid to your body.

Obvious or not, the results of these choices are the same both to you and to the people around you – no one feels engaged in the work or connected to each other, both of which are essential elements needed to foster team trust and build an innovative, productive (and enjoyable) environment.

YES, THIS IS ABOUT MULTITASKING

Multitasking is when you do more than one thing at the same time – in some cases, a handful of things at the same time. Several research studies have shown that multitasking is a waste of time because it divides attention, therefore decreasing both the quality of work and quality of experience.

Some researchers go so far as to say that there is no such thing as multitasking – only task-swapping, as the brain cannot perform two (or more) functions from the same area at the same time, so it goes back and forth.

Multitasking can double the amount of time it takes to complete a task, compared to focusing and completing a single task at a time. (Hint: multitasking is another way of distracting yourself that is not so obvious.)

IT'S NOT JUST MULTITASKING

There is also a growing inability within many corporate cultures to simply stop, think, see, and listen to what is happening within the environment, within working relationships, and within each individual.

The struggle for individuals, managers, and leaders to stop, think, see, and listen has grown over time due to many of the increasing demands from the world. Economic instability, limited resources (of time, money, people, natural), and the "new normal" workplace mentality of perfectionism at all costs is mixed with the drive for professional heroism.

IT'S NOT REVOLUTIONARY

Practicing presence, finding engagement, and creating connection is about getting back to the basics and practicing techniques that have worked for years. (Many, many years before mobile devices, computers, and electricity were even invented.)

The basics begin with STOP. Pause in the parade of busy and take a moment to THINK, "Why am I doing this, why now?" SEE your behavior and the impact it has on others, and then intentionally shift behaviors needed to support your desired outcomes. LISTEN: Really hear what is being communicated in words and actions; listen for what is expressed and what is repressed.

The real rebellion is that of choice. Choice to pause, reflect, see, and hear the world around you – choice to practice presence.

WHAT IS AROUND YOU?

Your environment is the surrounding things, conditions, and influences in which you exist each day. As it applies to the workplace, your environment is the physical setting in which work occurs.

The physical workplace environment includes things like your actual office building, your workspace (if you have an assigned workplace), the way your office feels, the view outside of your window (if you have a window), the smell of the room, and so on.

For many, work does not mean an actual workspace, but can be any place where a device is turned on or a work thought is occurring. If you are a flexible space/mobile worker, your physical surrounding can be a coffee shop, a room in your home, a co-working space, a café, or perhaps even a train or bus.

Whether you have an actual office or just a laptop, it is obvious that you are not immune to the distractions of your physical environment. What is not so obvious is when you experience total disengagement from your environment.

For example, ignoring the pile of paperwork on your desk to the point that you no longer see it, the squeaky chair you sit in or the loud person sitting next to you that you no longer hear, or the long-forgotten broken printer down the hall that may or may or may not be fixed by now.

For many people, the technology is or has become the whole job, so in many ways, technology can be a whole environment in and of itself.

A common struggle working professionals share from country to country is the struggle to manage the technology within our environments. Central to this is managing your relationship with mobile devices, including phones, laptops, and tablets as well as all the related applications and software.

The proliferation of digital devices in our environments is both a blessing and a curse. The computing power we hold in our pockets is astounding and can truly create and support deeper human connection and engagement, as well as wildly improve productivity and efficiency.

On the flip side, and equally astounding, is the power of these devices to create interruption in our lives and sabotage connections with others, with yourself, and even with the quality of your work.

QUESTIONS TO CONSIDER

Where are you and what is around you?

How does the space feel – is it open, closed, hot, cold?

Is there anything you can do to improve this space to support your needs?

Notice how many devices you use each day and which one for which purpose.

How often are your devices with you?

Do you use your devices when others are talking to you or when you are participating in a meeting?

What would your day be like if you limited technology interruptions?

Why do you use which technology when you do?
(For example, a text or instant message vs. a phone call.)

What have others said to you about how often and when you use your devices?

What do you say to yourself when you reach for a device or social media tool?

ACTIONS TO PRACTICE

When you enter a space, notice the details and how it feels.

When you enter a space, notice the technology around you.

Create technology-free time zones each day – for example, at meals or meetings.

Define what technology you will use for various types of communication.

Explore limiting the number of devices used at the same time.

Ask others to put their devices away when you are talking or leading a meeting.

PRACTICING PRESENCE WITH YOUR SURROUNDINGS IS ABOUT **BECOMING AWARE** OF WHAT YOU DON'T SEE EACH DAY, THAT INCLUDES YOUR **PHYSICAL SPACE** AS WELL AS THE **TECHNOLOGY** WITHIN THESE SPACES.

IT'S PRIMAL

Humans share a primal need for love and acknowledgment. We all yearn to be seen, to be heard, to be noticed. This basic human desire does not go away once we join a company or set foot into a work environment.

Somewhere along the journey something happens – we get distracted, get busy, and begin to operate from a place of time starvation. We micromanage our days, tasks, and activities, and the importance of these primal human needs fades.

It's true that we don't go to work to have our needs for love meet, but our need for acknowledgement is very important in the place where many of us spend most of our time. It's almost impossible to acknowledge one another and the work that is being done if we don't actually see and hear each other.

Human connection is the casualty of modern-day time demands, and this is a really big deal – because no company can survive, let alone thrive, without trusting stable relationships to drive work and generate innovation.

Relationship building is not only essential to building a strong team foundation, it is essential to our core primal needs. When people are connected, the environment is rich with creativity, innovation, efficiency, and togetherness.

If you are in a situation where teams and people are not connected at work, know that the large majority of people are not ill meaning or purposely trying not to connect. In most cases, they are just stuck in "busy" mode and unaware of how to actually be present with others. Being present is something people are not used to practicing and a skill that many have not seen modeled.

QUESTIONS TO CONSIDER

How often do you make eye contact with people at work?

What are the things you notice most about your peers? What they wear, how they make you feel, how they do their work?

Do you talk to people you work with about anything non–work related?

How much do you really know about the people you spend time with at work?

Are you able to be vulnerable and share with others about your life and feelings, about work and non-work experiences?

How often do you really hear what a person has just told you? Do you listen to the point where you understand how they are feeling as they share with you?

When someone speaks, how often do you let go of thinking about what you are going to say back, and just hear them?

Notice a person's body language – do their actions match their words while they are sharing?

Do you create a space that makes others feel heard – one with no distractions or interruptions (technology or otherwise)?

Do you jump right into a conversation, or make sure the other person is finished sharing?

ACTIONS TO PRACTICE

Make eye contact when you talk to people.

Let go of what you are thinking about when someone is talking to you; really hear what they are saying and notice what they are not saying.

Slow down the speed of conversation. Allow spaces in order to breathe, digest, and reflect on what is being said and not said.

Ask opened ended questions to generate deeper conversation, understanding and empathy.

Pay attention to what your body is doing and feeling when you are in conversation with others. Notice what is occurring as you talk and as you listen.

Reflect back and acknowledge what the other person is communicating to validate you understood the content of their message.

BUILDING PRESENCE

IN RELATIONSHIPS BEGINS WITH

SLOWING DOWN LONG ENOUGH

TO ACTIVELY LISTEN TO EACH OTHER'S WORDS

AS WELL AS

SEE EACH OTHER'S ACTIONS

WHEN THERE ARE NO WORDS SPOKEN.

TAMING THE INTERNAL CHATTER

It is much easier to practice presence and engagement with your environment and with others. In contrast, the most difficult place to practice presence is within.

The reality is that the modern world has wired us for internal disengagement. It is much, much easier to allow interruptions and distractions into our world than to feel our feelings, hear our authentic thoughts, and allow our truest selves to be expressed in words and actions.

Many people fear the calm and quiet of a still mind or a silent room, simply because they don't know what they will find when the chatter and distractions dissolve.

Fear of the unknown is natural fear. However, we are talking about you here, and you are hardly unknown to yourself. It might be reassuring to know there is no wrong way to begin to practice presence from within. There is no wrong way to be with your body, your thoughts, and yourself. There is only the way that is right for you.

For some, this may be a meditation cushion, a yoga mat, a running trail, a musical instrument, a paintbrush or pen, a walk with a pet, a bubble bath, cooking, sewing, gardening – the possibilities are endless.

QUESTIONS TO CONSIDER

How often do you create time for yourself?

How does your body feel?

When you have time for yourself, what distractions are around you and why?

What is your body doing and how is it feeling when you create time for yourself?

What is the emotion you are having connected to your thoughts?

Where do you feel conversations in your body?

How fast are your thoughts; do you feel the space between them?

How often do you really hear the thoughts in your head and reflect on their validity?

How often do you listen to yourself and follow your own coaching?

Does your language – what you say to yourself and others – match your actions?

Do you say the same things over and over to yourself? (Why do you think that is?)

ACTIONS TO PRACTICE

Create a self-check-in each day to listen to your mind and body (as little as three minutes will do).

Let go of what you are thinking that is not based on fact or truth.

Feel the impact of a conversation in your body before you think of your response.

Slow down the speed of your thoughts, or maybe pause thinking altogether for a few moments, trusting that all your thoughts will be there later when you are ready to resume thinking.

Experiment with silence, what does a quiet car or home feel like?

Breath. Practice paying attention to your breath. Look for when you are holding breath, taking short breaths and when you experience long deep breaths.

PRACTICING PRESENCE WITH SELF LOOKS DIFFERENT FOR EACH PERSON, BUT STARTS THE SAME WAY: BY MAKING THE CHOICE TO **CONNECT TO WHAT IS INSIDE.**

PRACTICE

DISRUPTING THE PATTERN

Here's the good news: You can link practicing presence to your habitual patterns, and make presence a habit in your life. A habit is a repeated behavior/action that may be conscious and/or unconscious – meaning that you can consciously create a habit.

On average, it takes about 60 days to create a new habit (although it could take as little as 20 days or as much as 300 days).

A habit is made up of three elements many call the "habit loop." It is comprised of a cue, followed by a routine behavior, then a reward.

The new routine must be repeated enough times so the brain can see the pattern and wire it into a habit.

It's possible that creating presence at work could be as simple as creating new habits to support presence with your environment, with others, and with yourself.

DEVELOPING A PRESENCE HABIT: ENVIRONMENT

What is ONE habit you want to createto help you be more present with your physical or technological environment?

Cue/trigger

Routine/behavior

Reward/desired outcome

What do you need to create this habit?

DEVELOPING A PRESENCE HABIT: RELATIONSHIPS

What is ONE habit you want to create to help you be more present in your relationships?

Cue/trigger

Routine/behavior

Reward/desired outcome

What do you need to create this habit?

DEVELOPING A PRESENCE HABIT: SELF

What is ONE habit you want to create to help you be more present with yourself?

Cue/trigger

Routine/behavior

Reward/desired outcome

What do you need to create this habit?

You will flow in and out of presence and experience different levels of presence your entire life.

There is no wrong place to begin to stop, think, see, and listen to the world around you. There is only the choice to begin to be more present.

THE CHOICE IS YOURS.

MINDFUL THOUGHTS...

MINDFUL THOUGHTS...

MINDFUL THOUGHTS...

MINDLESS THOUGHTS...

ABOUT THE AUTHOR

After years in senior communication roles, working countless hours crafting content for executives at Microsoft, Jae collapsed from stress-related adrenal fatigue directly attributed to the way she was living her life. This life-altering experience propelled Jae deep into research on human behavior, neuroscience, mindfulness, and organizational relationship systems.

In 2008, Jae founded WLB Consulting Group and developed the Mindful Life Program, which includes four group coaching workshops to generate reflection, awareness, and action at the organizational and individual levels.

Jae has taught work-life awareness workshops to thousands of employees at Microsoft and other technology companies in more than 50 countries including China, Russia, India, Japan, Brazil, Argentina, United Arab Emirates, France, Germany, United Kingdom, Norway, Sweden, Canada, and the United States.

Jae has an extensive background in writing and communication with a master's degree in Communication Management from Colorado State University and a bachelor's degree in Broadcast Communication from Metropolitan State College of Denver. She holds certificates in co-active coaching and organizational relationship systems coaching and is the author of seven books.

OTHER BOOKS BY JAE ELLARD

The Five Truths about Work-life Balance is about moving past the misconceptions surrounding work, life, and balance.

The Pocket Coach: Perspective When You Need Some is a book of questions to help you make clear choices.

Success with Stress is about five proactive choices you can make to reduce stress.

THE MINDFUL LIFE COLLECTION

Stop & Think: Creating New Awareness is about the choices you have and the understanding of the impact of the choices you make.

Stop & See: Developing Intentional Habits is about your ability to consciously choose to create habits that support your definitions of balance and success.

Stop & Listen: Practicing Presence is about working with your choices to create deeper engagement with self, others and your environment.

Beyond Tips & Tricks: Mindful Management is about leading groups to take accountability for making and accepting choices.

Created by Jae Ellard

Edited by Jenifer Kooiman

Designed by Hannah Wygal

Stop and Listen: Practicing Presence, 1st edition

2011-2014 Copyright by Simple Intentions

ISBN 978-0-9828344-9-7

Simple Intentions is a conscious content company working to increase awareness in the
workplace. For more information please visit www.simpleintentions.com.

Made in the USA
San Bernardino, CA
20 March 2017